DESIGNS
&
ORNAMENTS
FROM THE CHAPELS OF
Notre Dame

DESIGNS
&
ORNAMENTS
FROM THE CHAPELS OF

Notre Dame

EUGÈNE-EMMANUEL VIOLLET-LE-DUC

✠

MAURICE OURADOU

DOVER PUBLICATIONS, INC.
Mineola, New York

Copyright

Copyright © 2011 by Dover Publications, Inc.
All rights reserved.

Bibliographical Note

Designs and Ornaments from the Chapels of Notre Dame, first published by Dover
Publications, Inc., in 2011, is a republication of images from *Peintures Murales des
Chapelles de Notre-Dame de Paris,* published by A. Morel, Paris, in 1870. A Publisher's
Note has been written specially for this edition.

Library of Congress Cataloging-in-Publication Data

Viollet-le-Duc, Eugène-Emmanuel, 1814–1879.
    [Peintures murales des chapelles de Notre-Dame de Paris. English]
    Designs and ornaments from the chapels of Notre Dame / Eugène-Emmanuel
Viollet-le-Duc and Maurice Ouradou.
       p. cm.
    Originally published: Peintures murales des chapelles de Notre-Dame de Paris.
Paris : A. Morel, 1870.
    ISBN-13: 978-0-486-84050-5
    ISBN-10: 0-486-84050-6
    1. Viollet-le-Duc, Eugène-Emmanuel, 1814–1879—Themes, motives. 2.
Notre-Dame de Paris (Cathedral) 3. Church decoration and ornament—France—
Paris—History—19th century. I. Ouradou, Maurice, 1822–1884. II. Title.

NK2192.F84V566 2011
726.50944'361—dc22

                                    2010047040

Manufactured in the United States by LSC Communications
84050601   2019
www.doverpublications.com

Publisher's Note

One of the masterpieces of world architecture, the Cathedral of Notre Dame as it exists today is the culmination of countless renovations. Located on the Ile de la Cité—the medieval island within Paris regarded as the city's center—Notre Dame was constructed near the site of Saint Stephen's cathedral. Saint Stephen's was built between the fourth and seventh centuries (excavations have failed to determine the original date), following the transition from pagan worship to the establishment of Christianity in the region.

In the mid-twelfth century, with the election of Maurice de Sully as the bishop of Paris, a decision was made to build another cathedral near Saint Stephen's. Paris was growing in influence, and erecting a larger, more elaborate cathedral would reflect the importance of the city. Saint Stephen's would be demolished to make way for the new building. Drawing upon the medieval gothic style, builders during the twelfth and early thirteenth centuries added to the original plan a choir with a high altar, side aisles and tribunes in the nave, towers on the façade, and side chapels in the nave; the installation of stained glass and paintings added color to the cathedral. The lack of light within the building led to the enlarging of the windows—the darkness was thus relieved, and a more "modern" illumination was achieved. Although the first builder remains anonymous, later contributors to the construction include Jean de Chelles and Pierre de Montreuil. In many cases, designs begun by one architect were altered by his successor, and de Montreuil, who followed de Chelles, was more highly regarded for his contributions.

Additional developments in the late thirteenth and early fourteenth centuries included the construction of the choir chapels and the placement of a stone screen around the choir. During the seventeenth and eighteenth centuries (Notre Dame was by then in need of renovation), the sanctuary and choir were refurbished, and the stained glass windows, darkened with age, were replaced. Louis XIII, in 1638, believing his prayers to the Virgin to have been answered after his recovery from an illness, dedicated the cathedral to her. The French Revolution (late eighteenth century) brought its own changes to Notre Dame: numerous statues in the Gallery of Kings, as well as major portal statues, were destroyed, and the spire, dating from the thirteenth century, was removed.

Perhaps the most significant event to impact Notre Dame thereafter was the publication of *The Hunchback of Notre-Dame* (1831). It was already apparent that the cathedral was in need of repairs, and the grand success of Victor Hugo's novel led to a call for the restoration of the cathedral; ideally, restorations were to be made using original materials, and were to be consistent with the period. The formation of a committee in 1841 soon led to a full-blown campaign, which solicited plans from architects such as Jean-Jacques Arveuf, Jean-Baptiste Lassus,

Eugène-Emmanuel Viollet-le-Duc, and Jean-Charles Danjoy. Lassus and Viollet-le-Duc were chosen by the committee, and a budget was prepared. Work began in 1845; a new budget was required by 1850. After Lassus's death in 1857, Viollet-le-Duc took over the restoration. His contributions to the restoration of Notre Dame included the redesign of the outer chapel windows, the reconstruction of the spire above the crossing; the renovation of one of the enormous rose windows, which he designed to be exceptionally light-giving; the installation of paintings on the walls of the side chapels; and—a well-known feature of the cathedral—the addition of gargoyles and other decorative sculpted figures. In 1864, after extensive work and many cost overruns, the revamped Cathedral of Notre Dame was dedicated by the archbishop of Paris.

Eugène-Emmanuel Viollet-le-Duc, along with Maurice Ouradou, his son-in-law and the inspector of the renovations being carried out at Notre Dame, produced a compilation of designs and ornamental features of mural paintings in the cathedral's chapels. [The Plate numbers correspond to the Plan of Notre Dame that appears at the beginning of this book (Plate A)]. This splendid collection of images includes both abstract and representational elements, including Christian iconography. The motifs themselves range from floral patterns and charged animals to geometric designs, scrollwork, and checkerboards. Architectural details appear as well. A gargoyle can be located on Plate 26, echoing Viollet-le-Duc's role in adding the famed gargoyles to Notre Dame. Rich, harmonious colors inform each plate.

This masterwork of religious devotion and architectural genius stands today as a monument to the many builders—known and unknown—who gave developing Christianity a foothold in one of the world's great capitals.

List of Plates

DESIGNS
&
ORNAMENTS
FROM THE CHAPELS OF
Notre Dame

THE PLATES

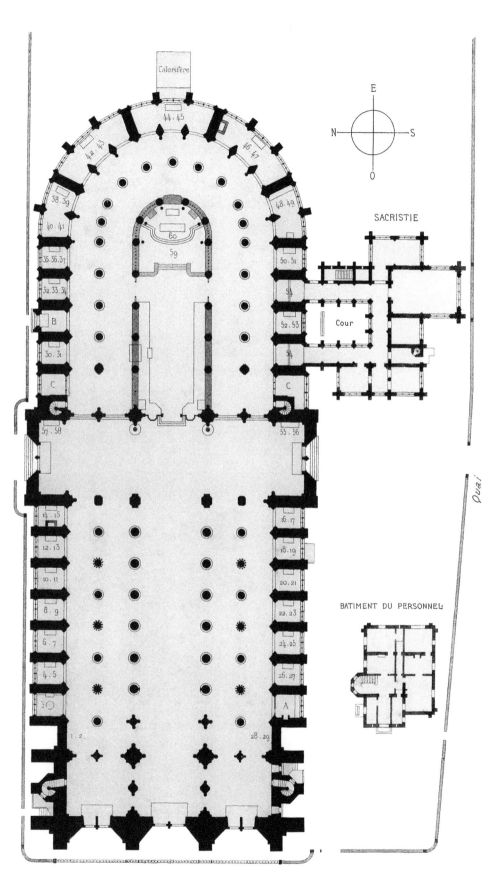

CHŒUR (côté nord)

30.31 .. Chapelle St Martin
32.33.34 .... " St Ferdinand
35.36.37 .... " St Germain
38 à 41 .... " St Louis
42.43 .... " St Marcel
        Chevet
44 45 . Chapelle N.D des sept douleurs

CHŒUR (côté sud)

46 . 47 . Chapelle St Georges
48 49 .... " St Guillaume
50 . 51 .... " Ste Madeleine
52 . 53 .... " St Denis
54 ... Passages de la Sacristie

B ..... Passage de la Porte-Rouge
C .... Débarras
        Sanctuaire
59 .... Tapis
60 .... id. de l'autel

55 . 56 Transept sud
57 . 58 Transept nord

NEF (côté nord)

1 . 2 .. Litanies de la Vierge
3 .... Chapelle des fonts Baptx
4 . 5 .... " St Charles
6 . 7 .... " de la Ste Enfance
8 . 9 .... " St Vincent de Paul
10 11 .... " St François Xavier
12 . 13 .... " St Landry
14 . 15 .... " Ste Clotilde

NEF (côté sud)

16 . 17 Chapelle du Sacré Cœur
18 . 19 .... " Ste Anne
20 . 21 .... " St Pierre
22 . 23 .... " St Joseph
24 . 25 .... " Ste Geneviève
26 . 27 .... " des âmes du Purgatoire
28 . 29 Christ (auréole)

A .... Chambre du Prédicateur

PLATE 1a

Plan de Notre Dame de Paris
Plan of Notre Dame of Paris

PLATE 1b

Detail d'une Chapelle de la Nef
Detail of a Nave Chapel

PLATE 1

Peinture derrière la Vierge
Painting behind the Virgin

PLATE 2

Peinture derrière la Vierge
Painting behind the Virgin

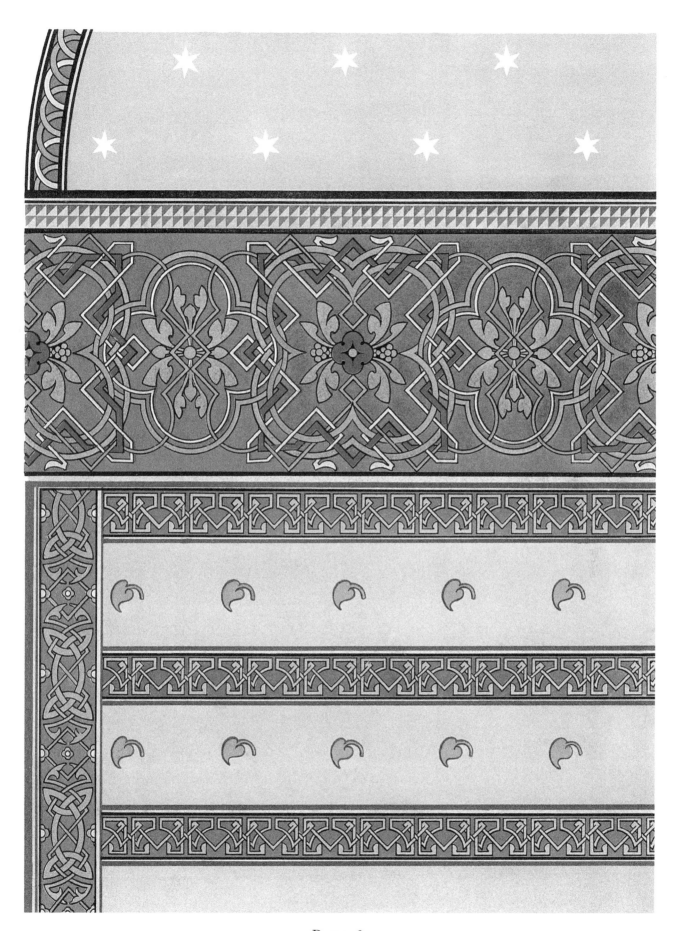

PLATE 3

Chapelle des Fonts Baptismaux
Chapel of Baptismal Fonts

Piher de l'autel

Motif au dessus de l'autel

Detail du Tabernacle

PLATE 4

Chapelle St. Charles
Saint Charles Chapel

Detail de la Piscine

PLATE 5

Chapelle St. Charles
Saint Charles Chapel

Motif au dessus de l'autel

Detail de la Piscine

LES ASSO
DE L'ŒUV
DE LA Sᵗᵉ EN
MDCCCLXV

PLATE 6

Chapelle de la Ste. Enfance
Chapel of the Children's Saint

Detail du soubassement

PLATE 7

Chapelle de la Ste. Enfance
Chapel of the Children's Saint

A ⋅ S^e ⋅ VINCENT
LES DAM€
DE ⋅ L'ŒVVRE ⋅ DES ⋅ PAVV
ⅯⅮⅭⅭⅭⅬⅩⅤ

PLATE 8

Chapelle St. Vincent de Paul
Saint Vincent de Paul Chapel

PLATE 9

Chapelle St. Vincent de Paul
Saint Vincent de Paul Chapel

PLATE 10

Chapelle St. François Xavier
Saint Francis Xavier Chapel

PLATE 11

Chapelle St. François Xavier
Saint Francis Xavier Chapel

PLATE 12

Chapelle St. Landry
Saint Landry Chapel

Tapisserie audessus de la 6.de fenêtre

Support de l'Autel

PLATE 13

Chapelle St. Landry
Saint Landry Chapel

PLATE 14

Chapelle Ste. Clotilde
Saint Clotilde Chapel

PLATE 15

Chapelle Ste. Clotilde
Saint Clotilde Chapel

PLATE 16

Chapelle du Sacre Cœur
Sacred Heart Chapel

PLATE 17

Chapelle du Sacre Cœur
Sacred Heart Chapel

Motif au dessus de l'autel

PLATE 18

Chapelle Ste. Anne
Saint Anne Chapel

Détail de la Piscine

Pilier du milieu

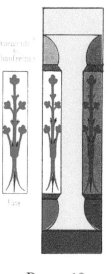

Ornements des Chanfreins

Face

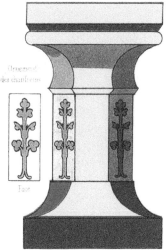

Ornement des chanfreins

Face

PLATE 19

Chapelle Ste. Anne
Saint Anne Chapel

PLATE 20

Chapelle St. Pierre
Saint Peter Chapel

Détail de la Piscine

Detail du retable en chêne à différents

face   coté

Angle d'encadrement

PLATE 21

Chapelle St. Pierre
Saint Peter Chapel

motif au dessus
de l'autel

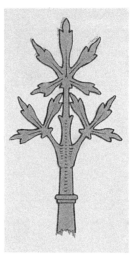

Fleuron

Pilier de l'autel

Détail de la Piscine.

PLATE 22

Chapelle St. Joseph
Saint Joseph Chapel

Angle supérieur d'encadrement

Detail du Tympan

PLATE 23

Chapelle St. Joseph
Saint Joseph Chapel

PLATE 24

Chapelle Ste. Geneviève
Saint Genevieve

NE DE PARIS
AMES
DE L'OEUVRE
NEVIEVE.

PLATE 25

Chapelle Ste. Geneviève
Saint Genevieve Chapel

Motif au dessus de l'autel

PLATE 26

Chapelle des Âmes du Purgatoire
Chapel of the Souls of Purgatory

O·SALVATORI
IRCATORIO·PATIENTEN
NTI·NOX·CORONANTI
SACRUO
MDCCCLXV

Pilier de l'autel

PLATE 27

Chapelle des Âmes du Purgatoire
Chapel of the Souls of Purgatory

PLATE 28

Peinture derrière le Crucifix
Painting behind the Crucifix

SIC · DEUS DILE

PLATE 29

Peinture derrière le Crucifix
Painting behind the Crucifix

PLATE 30

Chapelle St. Martin
Saint Martin Chapel

Détail du Soubassement

PLATE 31

Chapelle St. Martin
Saint Martin Chapel

PLATE 32

Chapelle St. Ferdinand
Saint Ferdinand Chapel

Mouf lateral   Motifs au dessus de l'Autel   Motif du milieu

PLATE 33

Chapelle St. Ferdinand
Saint Ferdinand Chapel

Détail de la Piscine sous la grande Fenêtre

PLATE 34

Chapelle St. Ferdinand
Saint Ferdinand Chapel

PLATE 35

Chapelle St. Germain
Saint Germain Chapel

Dessus de l'Autel

Detail de la croix de la pyramide.

Motif au dessus de l'Autel

peres ſubleuat ✠ B·Germanus' in cœlum aſſumitur ✠ B·Germanus Childebertum ſanat

PLATE 36

Chapelle St. Germain
Saint Germain Chapel

Décoration sous la grande fenêtre   Ornement développe de la colonne.

Détail du soubassement.

PLATE 37

Chapelle St. Germain
Saint Germain Chapel

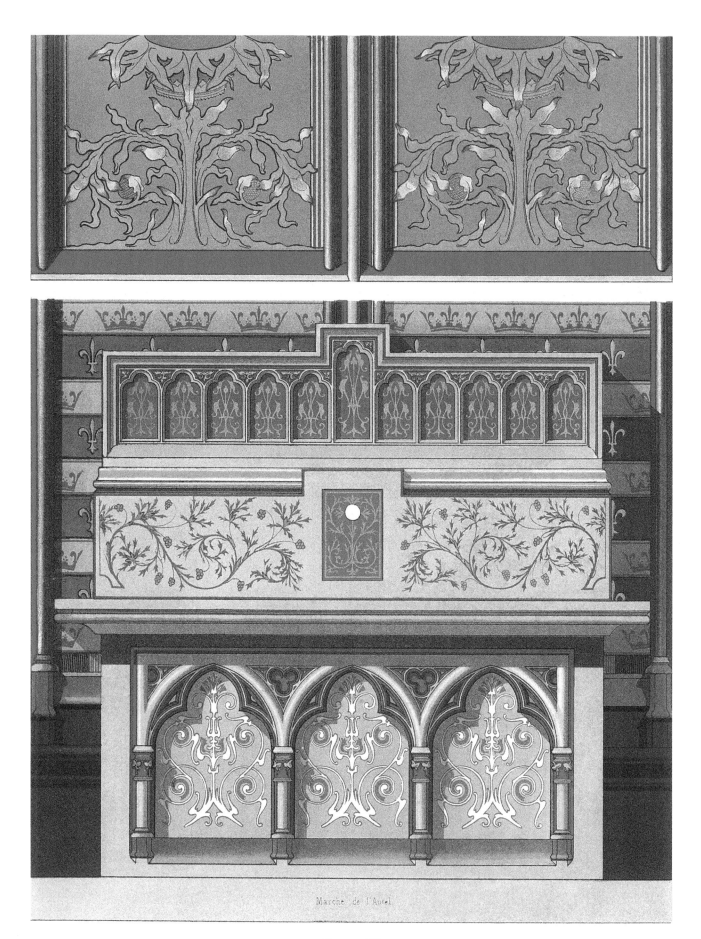

Marche de l'Autel

PLATE 38

Chapelle St. Louis
Saint Louis Chapel

PLATE 39

Chapelle St. Louis
Saint Louis Chapel

PLATE 40

Chapelle St. Louis
Saint Louis Chapel

Ornement au dessus des Figures

Coté au porch.

Ornement developpé sur les colonnes

Face de la piscine

PLATE 41

Chapelle St. Louis
Saint Louis Chapel

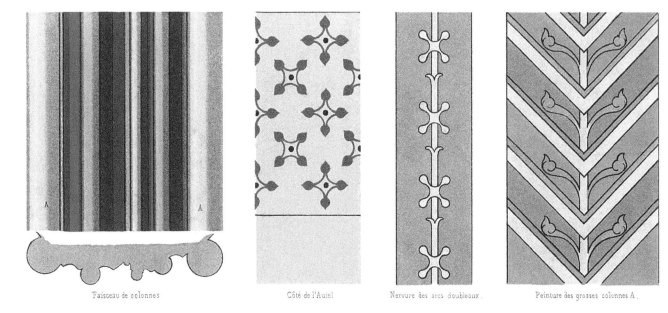

Faisceau de colonnes   Côté de l'Autel   Nervure des arcs doubleaux.   Peinture des grosses colonnes A.

Plate 42

Chapelle St. Marcel
Saint Marcel Chapel

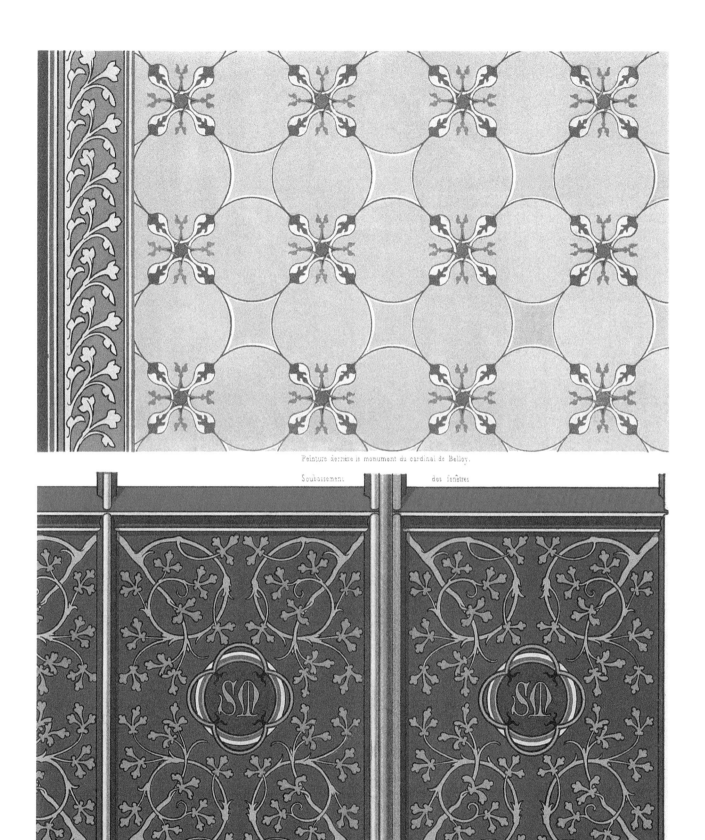

Peinture derrière le monument du cardinal de Bellov.

Soubassement   des fenêtres

PLATE 43

Chapelle St. Marcel
Saint Marcel Chapel

Ornement développé des colonnes A.   Bordure de l'arc doubleau   Bordure de l'arc doubleau

Ensemble d'un faisceau de Colonnes
A 20ᵐᵉ de l'exécution.

Plan du faisceau.

Ensemble de l'autel et du retable.

PLATE 44

Chapelle N. D. des Sept Douleurs
Chapel of the Seven Sorrows

Peinture d'une face latérale

Détail du soubassement   et de la Pierre

PLATE 45

Chapelle N. D. des Sept Douleurs
Chapel of the Seven Sorrows

Face latérale de l'Autel

Troisième piscine

Détail d'un pilier au 1/20

Ensemble de l'autel

PLATE 46

Chapelle St. Georges
Saint George Chapel

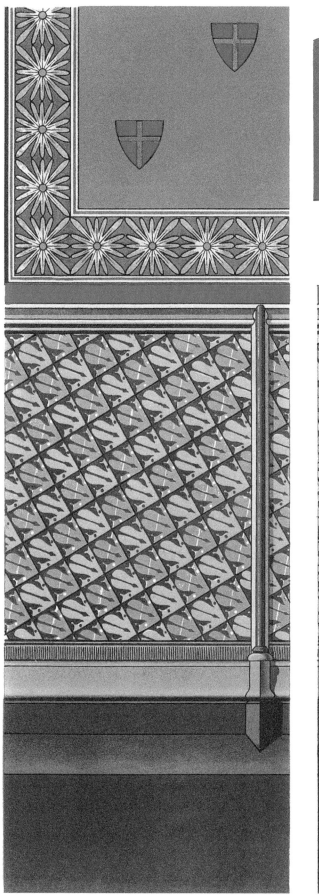

Détail de notre portion

Ornement développé sur les grosses colonnes

Détail d'une porte

PLATE 47

Chapelle St. Georges
Saint George Chapel

PLATE 48

Chapelle St. Guillaume
Saint William Chapel

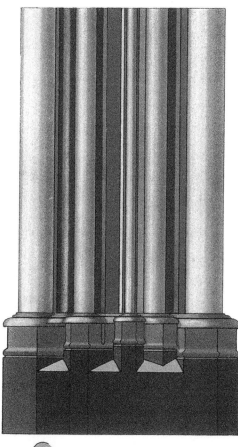

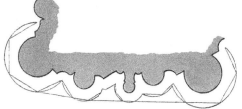

PLATE 49

Chapelle St. Guillaume
Saint William Chapel

Détail de l'Autel

Détail de la piscine sous la Grande fenêtre

PLATE 50

Chapelle Ste. Madeleine
Saint Madeleine Chapel

Ornem. développé sur les colonnes

Tapisserie au dessous de la fenêtre

Bordure au dessus du Soubassement

PLATE 51

Chapelle Ste. Madeleine
Saint Madeleine Chapel

PLATE 52

Chapelle St. Denis
Saint Denis Chapel

Détails du Ciborium au dessus de l'autel

PLATE 53

Chapelle St. Denis
Saint Denis Chapel

Divers
A Variety of Designs

PLATE 55

Transept Sud
South Transept

PLATE 56

Transept Sud
South Transept

Inscription

PLATE 57

Transept Nord
North Transept

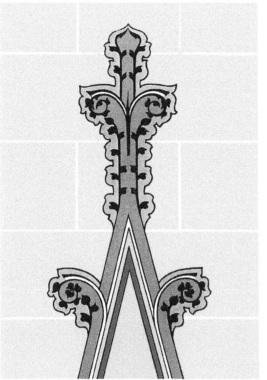

Détails des Pignons.

Soubassement.

PLATE 58

Transept Nord
North Transept

PLATE 59

Tapis du Sanctuaire
Sanctuary cloth

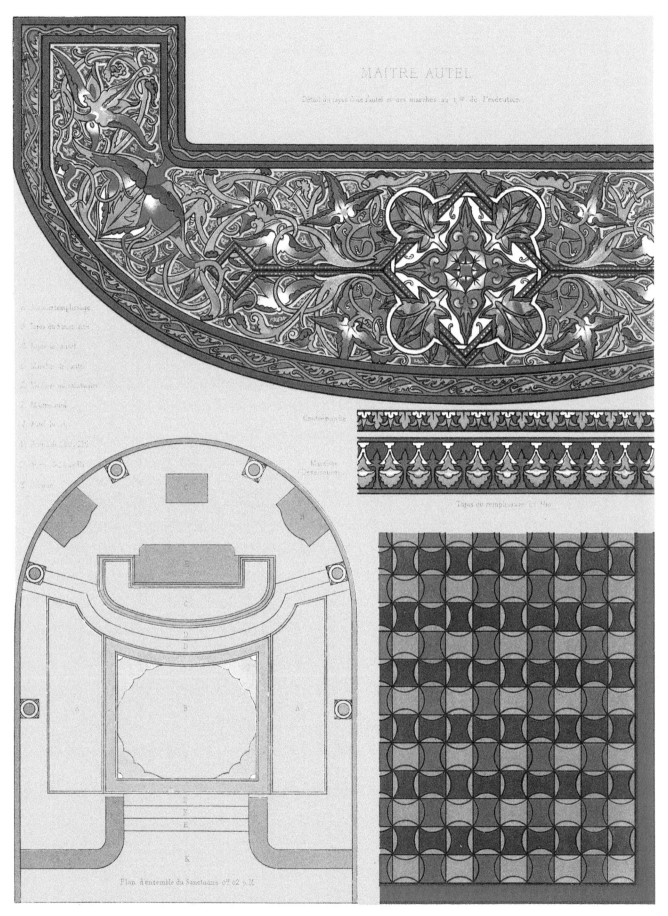

MAITRE AUTEL

Détail du tapis d'un l'autel et des marches au 1/10 de l'exécution

Plan d'ensemble du Sanctuaire 0.02 p.M

PLATE 60

Tapis de L'Autel
Altar cloth